T0042433

WORLD EXPLORERS

MISSIONS IN SPACE

— 1955–PRESENT —

Stephen Currie

PICTURE CREDITS
Cover (back), pages 2 (bottom), 3 (top left and bottom), 5 (bottom middle), 6, 7 (middle), 8 (top left), 14, 15, 16 (bottom), 19, 20, 21 (left), 21 (right), 22, 23, 27 (top right), 28, 29 (bottom), 30 (top left and right), 31 (bottom right) NASA; cover, pages 5 (middle), 9 (top), 27 (bottom) Bettmann/Corbis; page 1 Corbis; pages 4 (upper left), 4–5 (top), 16 (top left), 24 (top left), 24 (bottom), 25, 31 (top and bottom), 32 Photodisc; page 5 (top) Rykoff Collection/Corbis; page 5 (bottom right) U.S. Space & Rocket Center/DK Images; page 7 (left and right) Roger Ressmeyer/Corbis; pages 8 (bottom), 10, 11 (top and right), 12, 13, 26, 27 (top left) Sovfoto/Eastfoto; pages 18–19 NASA/Corbis; page 29 (bottom right) Reuters NewMedia Inc./Corbis.

Produced through the worldwide resources of the National Geographic Society, John M. Fahey, Jr., President and Chief Executive Officer; Gilbert M. Grosvenor, Chairman of the Board; Nina D. Hoffman, Executive Vice President and President, Books and Education Publishing Group.

PREPARED BY NATIONAL GEOGRAPHIC SCHOOL PUBLISHING
Ericka Markman, Senior Vice President and President, Children's Books and Education Publishing Group; Steve Mico, Vice President, Editorial Director; Marianne Hiland, Executive Editor; Anita Schwartz, Project Editor; Jim Hiscott, Design Manager; Kristin Hanneman, Illustrations Manager; Diana Bourdrez, Picture Editor; Matt Wascavage, Manager of Publishing Services; Lisa Pergolizzi, Sean Philpotts, Production Managers.

MANUFACTURING AND QUALITY MANAGEMENT
Christopher A. Liedel, Chief Financial Officer; Phillip L. Schlosser, Director; Clifton M. Brown III, Manager.

ART DIRECTION Dan Banks, Project Design Company

CONSULTANT/REVIEWER
Dr. Margit E. McGuire, School of Education, Seattle University, Seattle, Washington

BOOK DEVELOPMENT Nieman Inc.

BOOK DESIGN Three Communication Design, LLC

PICTURE EDITING AND MANAGEMENT
Corrine L. Brock
In the Lupe, Inc.

MAP DEVELOPMENT AND PRODUCTION Elizabeth Wolf

Published by the National Geographic Society
1145 17th Street, N.W.
Washington, D.C. 20036-4688

ISBN: 0-7922-4546-6

Printed in the USA
Fourth Printing March 2018

Cover: Astronaut F. Musgrave at the rear cargo hatch of Space Shuttle *Challenger*

page 1: *Gemini* rocket launch

page 2: *Apollo-Soyuz* mission patch

page 3 (top): *Gemini* capsule

page 3 (bottom): Buzz Aldrin walking on the moon

TABLE OF CONTENTS

THE WORLD IN 1955

By 1955, explorers had visited almost everywhere on Earth. It seemed as if there was only one more place to explore: space.

Space was not a complete mystery, of course. Scientists had studied the sun, moon, planets, and stars from Earth. There were lots of science-fiction books and movies about space. Still, no one had ever left the planet Earth to see what space was *really* like.

Another reason to explore space had to do with a rivalry between the United States and the Soviet Union. (The Soviet Union no longer exists. Today, most of its territory is the country of Russia.)

Both countries wanted new and better technology to spy on the other. For years, the two sides had similar weapons and technology.

Then, in 1957, the Soviets sent a **satellite** called *Sputnik* into space. Americans feared that the Soviets could spy or even launch attacks on the United States from space. The Americans hurried to strengthen their own space program. The "space race" had begun.

The race did not stop with satellites. Four years after *Sputnik,* the Soviets sent the first person into space, Yuri Gagarin (guh–GAR–in). Only eight years later, Neil Armstrong, an American, was the first person to walk on the moon.

Later, the space race changed. By 1975, the Soviets and Americans started working together on the joint *Apollo-Soyuz* mission. Competition in space became cooperation in space.

1957

4 ОКТЯБРЯ
в Советском Союзе произведен.
запуск ПЕРВОГО искусственного
СПУТНИКА ЗЕМЛИ

3 НОЯБРЯ
в Советском Союзе произведен.
запуск ВТОРОГО искусственного
СПУТНИКА ЗЕМЛИ

Postcard to celebrate
Sputnik launch

Sputnik

APOLLO/СОЮЗ

Neil
Armstrong's
walk on
moon

Yuri
Gagarin's
flight

Apollo-Soyuz
mission

Sputnik
launched

| 1955 | 1960 | 1965 | 1970 | 1975 | 1980 |

SPACESHIPS

Both the Soviet and the American space programs built their own spaceships. There are two important parts to a spaceship. The **capsule** is the section where **astronauts,** or space explorers, sit. Capsules are small and cramped, but they can travel quickly through space.

Capsules don't have the power to get past the **atmosphere,** the layer of gases surrounding Earth. For that, astronauts need **rockets,** vehicles with powerful engines. Rockets are thin and tall—sometimes taller than a 30-story building. They are usually divided into stages, or parts.

Scientists test rockets on the ground before launch.

VOSTOK **SATURN V** **A SPACE SHUTTLE**

Each stage contains at least one powerful engine. When the engine on one stage runs out of fuel, a new engine takes over. At the same time, the old stage drops off the rocket in order to save weight. The lighter the spaceship, the faster it will fly, and the less fuel it will need.

These pictures show three of the most famous rockets in the history of space travel. *Vostok* launched the first person in space. The *Saturn V* took crews to the moon. Solid rocket boosters launch space shuttle missions. The boosters are the two white rockets on the sides of the space shuttle.

FIRST PERSON IN SPACE

The first person in space was a Russian pilot named Yuri Gagarin. Yuri had wanted to be a pilot from the time he was small. He loved to watch military planes fly over the farm where he had been born in 1934. The men at the controls were "brave and handsome," he remembered years later. Yuri wanted to be just like them.

As he grew older, Gagarin kept his fascination with planes. He took flying lessons in college and made his first solo flight at age 21. That flight, he said, "gave meaning to my whole life." Before long, Gagarin joined the Soviet Air Force. He had achieved his dream. Then, in 1957, the Soviet Union launched *Sputnik*. Suddenly, flying was no longer enough.

Gagarin was caught up in the mystery and excitement of space. When he heard that the Soviets were starting a program to train **cosmonauts**—the Russian word for space explorers—he was thrilled. He asked to join the program, and he was accepted.

Yuri Gagarin

There was only one problem: government officials would not let Gagarin talk about what he was doing. No one could talk about the space program. The Soviets didn't want the Americans to know they were training cosmonauts, so they kept the program a secret. Gagarin's parents thought he was still flying planes. Even his wife, Valentina, did not know all the details.

Model of Gagarin's rocket, now ▶ on display in Moscow

North Pole

ARCTIC OCEAN

SOVIET UNION

Moscow

Landing Site

Black Sea

Caspian Sea

Aral Sea

Baikonur Cosmodrome (SOVIET LAUNCH CENTER)

Kilometers
0   1000

Miles
0   1000

N
W   E
S

Yuri Gagarin's Mission
Around the World, 1961

AROUND THE WORLD IN 108 MINUTES

The first flights in space were not going to be easy. The capsules were cramped. They might be brutally hot or ice cold. There might be strange noises and flashing cockpit lights when the cosmonauts were trying to concentrate. Most difficult of all, the cosmonauts would be weightless in space. Soviet scientists thought about these problems when they trained the cosmonauts.

Gagarin spent hours in a small, hot room to get used to the cramped spaceship. Machines whipped him back and forth, showing him how it might feel during launch. Gagarin practiced solving math problems while trainers distracted him with noise and lights. The cosmonauts' training prepared them both physically and mentally for space travel.

Gagarin's trainers were impressed. They called him "bold" and "decisive," and they chose him to be the first man in space. Gagarin's task was to **orbit**—to travel around—Earth. Just after 9 o'clock on the morning of April 12, 1961, his spaceship, *Vostok I,* took off with a roar. Gagarin was shot through Earth's atmosphere and into space.

Gagarin swept around Earth at the speed of five miles (eight kilometers) per second. He was traveling so fast that the flight lasted just 108 minutes. Still, Gagarin made sure to look out the window at Earth, spinning miles below him. "I can see the clouds," he reported. "I can see everything. It's beautiful!" His view of Earth did not last long. Soon, his capsule rotated into position to reenter the atmosphere and land in the Soviet Union.

Gagarin's capsule in a field

As Gagarin approached the Soviet Union, his capsule began to descend. Gagarin ejected from the ship and used a parachute to float gently to Earth. Some farmers found him in a field. "Have you come from outer space?" asked one woman. She was startled by his parachute and his orange flight suit. "I certainly have!" the cosmonaut replied.

◄ Gagarin aboard *Vostok I*

SOVIET HERO

Until April 12, hardly anyone had ever heard of Yuri Gagarin. Now, the first person in space was a national hero. On April 14, he flew to Moscow, the Soviet capital, for an official welcome. Government leaders unrolled a red carpet for him when his plane landed. Later, he noticed that his shoe had been untied when he walked down the carpet. Luckily, he didn't trip over the lace.

Among the important people who met Gagarin at the airport was Nikita Khrushchev (KROOSH-chef), the leader of the Soviet Union. Khrushchev shook Gagarin's hand. Then, the two men got into Khrushchev's car and headed to Red Square in the heart of Moscow. There, Gagarin and others gave speeches while thousands cheered.

Gagarin received many national awards. ▶

◀ Khrushchev, Yuri Gagarin, and his
wife parade through Moscow.

Overnight, Gagarin had become the most popular man in the Soviet Union. Soviet officials put up a monument to their hero and awarded him prizes for what he had done. The mood of the country was bright. A Soviet flier had gone into space. Anything seemed possible! The Soviet Union cheered, but the United States did not.

Americans were shocked when they heard about Gagarin's flight. First, the Soviets had launched *Sputnik*—and now this! The Americans seemed to be falling further and further behind in the space race. Even though the United States had to scramble to catch up, Americans were excited. At night, they could see spacecraft in the sky. It was amazing.

AMERICANS FOLLOW

Soon, the Americans started to draw even with the Soviets. Less than a month after Gagarin's adventure, an American military pilot named Alan Shepard rocketed into space aboard *Mercury 3*. Shepard did not circle Earth as Gagarin had done, and Shepard's flight lasted just 15 minutes. Still, the launch proved that the United States could send an astronaut into space.

Over the next few years, the space race became even tighter. The United States and the Soviet Union both poured money into their space programs. Each one tried to stay ahead of the other. Both countries were eager to be first and best. Sometimes, the Soviets seemed to be ahead. Other times, Americans took the lead.

John Glenn, the first American to orbit Earth, is launched in 1963.

By 1964, the Soviets had learned how to send two or three men up in a spaceship at the same time. Within a year, the United States could do that too. In March 1965, a Soviet cosmonaut left the space capsule in a special suit that allowed him to breathe. This was called a "space walk." Three months later, American Ed White made a space walk of his own— and stayed out of the capsule longer.

With every flight, spacecrafts got faster and better. Astronauts started spending days in space. In 1961, it had seemed amazing just to send Yuri Gagarin into orbit for almost two hours. By the late 1960s, it was clear that people could do much, much more. This space race would not end until someone had put a human being on the moon.

Ed White floats outside his capsule in 1965.

CHAPTER 2

THE MOON RACE

The American given the job of piloting to the moon was Neil Armstrong. Armstrong was born in 1930 in Wapakoneta, Ohio. Like Yuri Gagarin, Armstrong was interested in airplanes when he was a boy. He took his first airplane ride at age six. He had his pilot's license before he learned to drive a car.

Neil Armstrong studied engineering in college. He wanted to learn how to design planes as well as how to fly them. Still, flying was what he did best. "He flies an airplane like he's wearing it," remarked one friend. So, Armstrong decided to be a pilot.

During the early 1950s, Armstrong flew 78 military missions in the Korean War. Later, he was a test pilot for new airplanes. Some of the jets he flew could reach speeds of 4,000 miles (6,400 kilometers) an hour.

Neil Armstrong

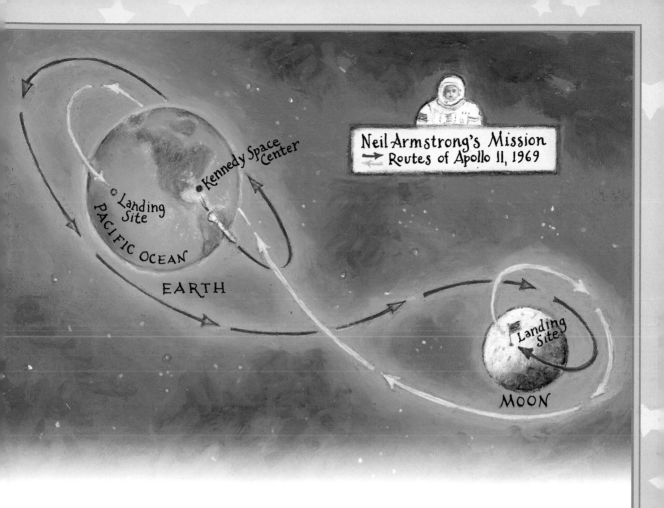

Neil Armstrong's Mission
→ Routes of Apollo 11, 1969

Kennedy Space Center

Landing Site

PACIFIC OCEAN

EARTH

Landing Site

MOON

In 1962, Armstrong joined the space program. Not only was he an excellent pilot, but he seemed able to stay calm no matter what was happening around him. His first space flight proved it. In 1966, he was piloting *Gemini 8* with astronaut David Scott when all at once the craft started spinning wildly. "We've got serious problems here," Armstrong told the **ground crew**.

The support staff on Earth could do nothing to help. Armstrong and Scott were on their own. Trying not to get too dizzy as *Gemini* spun, they checked everything that might be wrong. At last, they found an important control that wasn't working and fixed the problem. *Gemini* recovered—and brought them home safely.

JOURNEY TO THE MOON

In 1969, American space officials decided they were ready to send a crew to the moon. They named three astronauts who would make the journey. Armstrong was made commander of the mission, which was called *Apollo 11*. If all went well, he would be the first person to set foot on the moon. Edwin "Buzz" Aldrin and Michael Collins would join Armstrong on the flight.

On July 16, the three astronauts prepared to take off from the Kennedy Space Center in Florida. The three men sat in a small space capsule at the top of the *Saturn V*, the biggest rocket ever built at the time. *Saturn V* had five engines and weighed over six million pounds (2,700,000 kilograms) at liftoff. On the morning of the 16th, Armstrong, Aldrin, and Collins blasted off.

Michael Collins took a picture of the *Eagle* above the moon.

The moon was about 240,000 miles (384,000 kilometers) away. This is a distance more than ten times greater than the distance around Earth. The rocket was very powerful. Still, it took Armstrong and his crew just three days to make the journey. Their spacecraft orbited 60 miles (96 kilometers) above the surface of the moon. The astronauts prepared for their next step.

At this point, the astronauts split up. Armstrong and Aldrin entered the *Eagle*, a small spacecraft called a **lunar module**, while Collins stayed in the main capsule. On July 20, Armstrong and Aldrin detached the *Eagle* from the rest of the ship. Slowly, the *Eagle* made its way down toward the surface of the moon.

Saturn V spacecraft

ACROSS CULTURES

The Soviets also tried to launch moon missions, but their program never took off. One reason is that they never had a rocket as powerful as the Saturn V. The Soviet designers thought that the Saturn V was too big and too complex to work correctly.

"THE *EAGLE* HAS LANDED"

Armstrong and Aldrin needed a flat place to land their module, but they had trouble finding one. The surface of the moon seemed very rough. For a while, Armstrong wondered if they might have to go back without landing. The *Eagle* did not carry much fuel, and they could not afford to spend much time looking for a good landing place.

Luck was with the astronauts. Several minutes before they would have had to turn around, they saw a flat stretch of land. Armstrong set the module down near a pile of rocks. The ship settled into the powdery soil of the moon's surface. Then Armstrong radioed a message back to Earth. "The *Eagle* has landed," he said.

Aldrin stands by the American flag on the moon.

There was more to come. Millions of people were watching on television all around the world when Armstrong opened the door of the *Eagle*. Dressed in a spacesuit, Armstrong climbed slowly down a ladder and set one foot firmly on the surface of the moon. "That's one small step for man," Armstrong said, "one giant leap for mankind."

During the next two hours, Armstrong and Aldrin explored the area where they had touched down. The moon's low **gravity** let them take giant steps when they walked. Luckily, their training had prepared them for it. They did some experiments, gathered rocks, and set up an American flag. Then, they boarded the *Eagle* and blasted off to rejoin Collins. The blast from the engines blew the flag over.

TRAVELERS' TALES

As Neil Armstrong climbed down the ladder from the Eagle to the moon, he was communicating with the ground crew on Earth. He had this to say about the surface of the moon: "[It's] very, very fine grained as you get close to it. It's almost like a powder." The surface was so soft that his feet sank an inch (2.5 centimeters) or more into it.

21

BACK HOME

On July 24, 1969, the astronauts' capsule landed safely in the Pacific Ocean. Armstrong, Aldrin, and Collins were met by a helicopter. It flew them to a ship where space program officials were waiting. Armstrong, Aldrin, and Collins were not yet through with their journey.

The astronauts might have picked up some strange disease while on the moon. It would be a disaster if germs from the moon got loose on Earth! So, the men spent 18 days away from everyone else while scientists and doctors checked them for signs of illness. Then the astronauts were free to join their families.

◄ President Richard Nixon visited the astronauts.

Space program officials congratulated the crew. The Soviets had launched the first astronaut and had made the first space walk, but the Americans took the grand prize. The United States had won the moon race. To this day, it remains the only country to have sent an astronaut to the moon.

The lunar rover rode like a buggy on the moon.

Over the next three years, American astronauts visited the moon five more times. Some of these trips used a **lunar rover**— a vehicle built to travel across the surface of the moon. One astronaut even hit a few golf balls. All of these flights taught us more about the moon. All of them brought more moon rocks and more soil samples back to Earth. Since 1972, no human being has set foot on the moon.

CHAPTER 3

OPENING SPACE FOR ALL

In the burst of excitement that followed the moon landing, many people believed the next major mission would send an astronaut to Mars. Others thought there would be space stations by the year 2000. Instead, space scientists have turned their attention to other ways of exploring space.

In May 1973, a spacecraft called *Skylab* blasted off from the Kennedy Space Center. *Skylab* was a space station built to stay in orbit for several years. Just as the name suggests, it was a science lab in the sky.

Over the next few years, different astronaut crews stayed at *Skylab* for weeks or even months at a time. Their job was not to visit other planets, but to carry out scientific experiments.

Skylab orbited Earth for six years.

Space shuttle *Endeavour* became
the newest space shuttle in 1991.

The experiments taught the people on *Skylab* a great deal about biology, chemistry, and other areas of science. For instance, they found that months of weightlessness made people lose much of their muscle strength. They investigated how plants grew in space, and they tried making medical devices in the space lab. Whatever the scientific question, *Skylab* was a place to find out the answer.

Skylab was replaced by other space stations. To carry passengers back and forth between the ground and these stations, scientists built special spacecrafts called space shuttles. The shuttles had room for lots of scientific equipment. Unlike earlier spaceships, the shuttles could be used again and again.

COOPERATION AND DIVERSITY

Now that science was more important than the space race, American and Soviet officials began to work together. In 1975, a Soviet *Soyuz* spaceship docked with an American *Apollo* ship in space. The two groups of astronauts shared a meal and did some experiments together before going their separate ways. Later, American officials invited Soviet astronauts to use their space stations.

Before long, astronauts from many nations were in space. Astronauts from Germany, England, Japan, and other nations took shuttles to the space stations to carry out experiments of their own. Their projects helped everyone, not just the citizens of those countries. Cooperation in space was working for the good of all.

Astronauts aboard the *Apollo-Soyuz* mission

(top left) Valentina Tereshkova
(bottom) Sally Ride
(right) Guion Bluford

At the same time, American astronauts were becoming more diverse. In 1983, Sally Ride flew aboard the shuttle *Challenger* and became the first American woman in space. (A Soviet cosmonaut, Valentina Tereshkova, had been the first woman in space back in 1963.) Later that year, Guion Bluford became the first African American in space.

Astronauts were changing in another way too. The first American astronauts had been military test pilots. By the early 1980s, that was no longer true. Now, astronauts were more likely to be scientists, chosen for their ability to set up and carry out important experiments aboard the space shuttle. More and more, space officials were opening space to new work and new people.

A DIFFICULT FRONTIER

Scientists and astronauts had shown that people could live and work in space for long periods of time. Still, space flight remained very dangerous. The shuttle is a very complicated vehicle with many parts. When things don't work properly, they are usually found and fixed before any damage is done. Sometimes, however, tragic accidents take place.

In January 1986, the shuttle *Challenger* exploded 73 seconds after takeoff. All seven astronauts aboard were killed. Among them was Christa McAuliffe, a social studies teacher from New Hampshire. She had been chosen to be the first teacher in space. In 2003, another explosion destroyed the shuttle *Columbia*, killing seven more astronauts.

◀ In training, Christa McAuliffe felt what it is like to be weightless in space.

In spite of the dangers, the space program has continued. In 1998, 16 countries joined together and began to build the International Space Station (ISS). Much of the construction took place in space! Although the station is not yet complete, it is already in use. When finished, ISS will weigh over one million pounds (454,000 kilograms) and have six separate science labs. Already, scientists can spend four months or more living and working aboard ISS.

In many ways, the experience aboard ISS is hard. Scientists are away from friends and family. The food can get boring very quickly. The low gravity of the station can make them weak and tired. Yet, the ISS scientists love doing the work they do. Their experiments help us all understand space better—and ourselves as well. With the opening of ISS, more people are working on space projects, and more people are traveling in space.

A space shuttle crew took this picture after unlocking from ISS.

A CONTINUING JOURNEY

The space program affects the lives of people everywhere. Scientific discoveries in space have improved human technology in everything from calculators to frying pans. Who knows what great discoveries may be next?

More countries want to have a part in space exploration. Some are even starting their own space programs. In fact, China launched its first space explorer, Yang Liwei, in 2003.

The space program has also been important in showing what can happen when people work together. Space exploration is no longer a contest. On the contrary, the international space station is an example of how countries can cooperate.

Finally, brave explorers like Gagarin, Armstrong, and the shuttle

An idea for what a Mars base might look like

astronauts have shown us what lies beyond our own planet. For years, people had dreamed of space. Now, through these men and women, we have all journeyed into the great unknown. The risks are many, but the rewards have been great. We can never again see our own world in quite the same way.

GLOSSARY

astronaut a space explorer

atmosphere the gases surrounding a planet or other body in space

capsule the part of a spacecraft where the space explorers ride

cosmonaut the Russian word for space explorer

gravity the force that holds things onto a body in space, such as a planet or moon

ground crew the support staff on Earth

lunar module the capsule designed to land on the surface of the moon

lunar rover a vehicle built to travel across the surface of the moon

orbit to travel around a planet or star

rocket a powerful vehicle with extremely strong engines

satellite an object, often made by humans, that circles a planet or a star

Space shuttle spacewalk

31

INDEX